WALTER JOHNSON

The Mind Power

Your Easy Manual For The World of Manipulation Secrets, With Tips and Tricks To Control People And Understand the Power Of Our Mind

Copyright © 2021 Walter Johnson

All rights reserved.

© **Copyright 2021 - All rights reserved.**

The content contained within this book may not be reproduced, duplicated or transmitted without direct written permission from the author or the publisher.

Under no circumstances will any blame or legal responsibility be held against the publisher, or author, for any damages, reparation, or monetary loss due to the information contained within this book. Either directly or indirectly.

Legal Notice:

This book is copyright protected. This book is only for personal use. You cannot amend, distribute, sell, use, quote or paraphrase any part, or the content within this book, without the consent of the author or publisher.

Disclaimer Notice:

Please note the information contained within this document is for educational and entertainment purposes only. All effort has been executed to present accurate, up to date, and reliable, complete information. No warranties of any kind are declared or implied. Readers acknowledge that the author is not engaging in the rendering of legal, financial, medical or professional advice. The content within this book has been derived from various sources. Please consult a licensed professional before attempting any techniques outlined in this book.

By reading this document, the reader agrees that under no circumstances is the author responsible for any losses, direct or indirect, which are incurred as a result of the use of information contained within this document, including, but not limited to, — errors, omissions, or inaccuracies.

Table of Content

Introduction 5
Chapter 1. The Dark Triad 11
Chapter 2. How To Analyze People 16
Chapter 3. Speed Reading to Understand People 24
Chapter 4. Advanced Tips and Tricks to Control People 32
Chapter 5. The Most Powerful Mind-Power Tool 38
Chapter 6. NLP 44
Chapter 7. Covert Manipulation 48
Chapter 8. What is Manipulation? 54
Chapter 9. Examples of Manipulation? 61
Conclusion 67

Introduction

When someone is trying to deceive another person, the intentions are usually going to be pretty bad. It is a useful tool for being a dark manipulator, but you have to remember that most people will not be happy if they find out it is being used against them.

Perceiving Deception

Suppose the subject is enthused about maintaining a strategic distance from deception in their life to keep up a key decent way from the mind games that go with it. In that case, it is as frequently as conceivable a sharp plan to understand how to recognize when deception is going on. Reliably, it is difficult for the subject to find that deception is going on, except for if the master goofs and lies are clear or noticeable, or they repudiate something that the subject undeniably knows to be genuine. While it might be difficult for the chairman to cheat the subject for an important stretch, it will, by and large, happen in typical ordinary nearness between people who know one another. Recognizing when deception happens is regularly hazardous, considering the path that there few pointers that are completely solid to tell when deception occurs.

Techniques Used in Deception

Deception is a type of expression that utilizes lies and omissions to persuade the victim to fit into the world that the agent wants. A form of interaction or communication has to be involved. Deception can manifest itself in different types, according to the situation where it is applied. It is challenging to tell when someone is trying to deceive others. Luckily, though, there are a few components that, when identified, point to the likelihood of deception being involved. After many years of studying deception, psychologists have developed three classifications of deception: camouflage, simulation, and disguise. Out of the three classifications of deception, we can identify the common techniques used in deception. Let us first define the classifications.

Camouflage

Camouflage is the first classification of deception. The deceiver works to conceal the truth of their intentions in a way that the subject cannot decode. Just like the typical camouflage deployed by animals and plants to hide from predators or to approach prey without being detected, deceivers make use of methods that are hard to detect without extra observation.

Simulation

The second classification of deception is simulation. Simulation is the act of imitating to be something. In deception, simulation is defined as exposing the victim to false information as a tool of misleading them. There are three types of simulation described below.

Fabrication

Fabrication means altering reality. The deceiver can use a real thing and change it to work in their favor. For example, they can add or reduce details to a story to make it better or worse to convince the subject. A real-life example is when a suspect in court over stealing tells the judge that they stole food because they were almost starving, yet they intended to sell their loot for financial gain.

Mimicry

The second type of simulation is known as mimicry. Mimicry is defined as the art of imitating to ridicule or confuse a situation. In deception, mimicry happens when the deceiver pretends to be something or someone that they are not. A deceiver might steal an idea from someone, and instead of citing the owner; they use it as their own. An example of mimicry is when an author uses a famous writer's name to fool readers to purchase their book.

Distraction

The final type of simulation is called distraction. Distraction is the act of cunningly forcing the victim to shift their attention from reality and focus on falsehood. To divert the subject, a deceiver can use a form of bait, which might appear to be more convincing or beneficial than the truth.

Disguise

The third classification of deception is a disguise. Disguise is defined as the act of faking a different appearance to conceal one's identity. When it is being deployed, the deceiver puts up the impression of being somebody or something different from what they are. Practically, disguise means the agent keeps something from the victim, as their intentions, what they do for a living, etc.

Lies

A lie refers to the agent's act in making up and feeding the victim information that is not true. When presenting a lie, the deceiver makes it appear as a fact, thereby making the subject absorb it as the truth. Lies are the most common techniques used in deception since they divert the victim from verifiable facts and make them easy targets of manipulation.

Concealment

Concealment is the act of preventing something from being recognized. In deception, it is mostly deployed by the use of half-truths. While giving information, the deceiver intentionally omits some essential parts to keep some truth from the receiver. While the deceiver will not have lied to the victim directly, they will have ensured that the most important information has been kept from them.

Creating Illusions

Deceivers are experts at creating convincing illusions. Once they have acquired the subject's attention, they demonstrate imaginary pictures that sway them into partnering with them. They come up with illusions that appear to be realistic and workable in every way. The first step of creating the illusions is to explain their "ideas" to the target's mind. After that, they pull back a little to wait and see if the subject will develop an interest in the illusions.

Equivocations

Waffling is the application of ambiguous language to hide the truth. Ambiguous language can be indirect or contradictory. The equivocations' objective is to confuse the victim, so they are not aware of what is happening. If a deceiver is asked a question, he avoids giving definite answers and provides general responses. They can also be used by the deceiver to escape blame if they are found out. If they are suspected, they give many explanations about whose aim is to confuse the accuser.

Understatements

An understatement is a situation that has been minimized but can cause more effects than what has been portrayed. The deceiver delivers a statement to their victim while making it appear like a small deal than what it is. However, the statement can influence the victim more than they have been made to believe.

Exaggeration

Exaggeration is the opposite of an understatement. It is whereby a situation is overstretched or overstated to alter it. The deceiver might not be lying directly to the victim, but they turn a situation into a far bigger deal than it is. Exaggerations can be used to convince the victim in a situation where they would not be, had they been given the genuine version of the situation.

Seduction

Seduction is typical on social media, where a person can write an attractive bio about themselves and top it up with carefully processed photos or videos to catch others' attention. The problem is that both the bio and the media provided by such people might be false and only intended to lure followers or lovers.

Rationalization

Rationalization is the deployment of weak or far-fetched arguments with the intent of convincing someone that something is more pleasant than it appears. In the context of deception, the agent comes up with clear ideas to convince the victim to do something difficult to accept or is unpleasant under normal circumstances.

Playing the Servant

Another method used to deceive people is playing the volunteer or servant role. In this case, the deceiver hides their agenda by making their victims believe that they are doing something for a noble cause. The subjects are less likely to suspect that someone is up to some mischief, who claims to be doing something to assist others. Therefore, they end up trusting them and concurrently lowering their defense mechanisms. Once the deceivers have their way, they unravel their evil plans.

Diversion

Diversion is the action of changing the natural or acceptable course of something. In deception, diversion is a tricky endeavor that aims at destroying a subject. Mind controllers are aware of the human traits which direct their responses, behaviors, and personalities, such as self-esteem and discipline.

Playing the Victim

Deception takes a lot of consideration for emotions. A deceiver uses playing victims to appear weaker or hurt, whereas they are the ones in control. The idea is to make others believe that they are victims of circumstances to evoke sympathy, compassion, and pity from the people they look forward to deceiving. Once a victim shows some form of concern for the deceiver, they cooperate with them and become easy to deceive.

Chapter 1. The Dark Triad

Often, abusers fall within this category—the dark triad. The dreaded three personality types combine to create a human storm capable of destroying lives so utterly that the individuals have little hope of reassembling them without intensive professional assistance. These personality types are dark—they do not care about people and encompass everything wrong, and everything toxic about humanity. They are often monstering within human skin, staring out into the world, and looking to wreak as much havoc as they can as quickly as possible. These three traits are Machiavellianism, narcissism, and psychopathy. They are dangerous enough on their own, but when you find an individual who harnesses them all, be forewarned—you are better off leaving while you still can and escaping all of the nonsense altogether as quickly as possible.

Machiavellianism

If you had to simplify Machiavellianism into the shortest possible phrase— "The ends justify the means." Though never directly stated by Niccolò Machiavelli, an Italian politician and philosopher from the 1500s, this phrase came from the text he wrote in The Prince in 1513. He informed the prince that was being instructed within the document to present himself in one way, honest and benevolent, even though he was ready to behave as harshly as necessary because everyone can see a person. But very few people will ever actually get close enough to realize the truth. The message is essentially summed up by saying that the ends justify the means, meaning that it was acceptable to lie because it made the prince more well-liked. A well-liked leader is far more likely to be a successful leader that can maintain power.

Drawing from that principle, Machiavellian people are adept at appearing how those around them wish to see them. They will say whatever those around them want to hear because they know that it is unlikely that those around them will ever know the truth, and telling them what they want to hear makes them happier and gets the Machiavellian person what he or she wants. Then, getting the desired result, the end justifies the means of lying, even though lying is typically considered morally wrong and reprehensible.

This personality type is quite insidious—you never know whether you see what you are getting. The Machiavellian individual is deceitful and a master at deceiving people around him or her. They will only tell the truth if it is beneficial to them or is the most desired result, which it usually is not. They assume that it is more important to seem desirable and make good connections than developing proper relationships. Still, when you see people as nothing more than a means to an end, you are not likely to ever want to develop a relationship with others. When people are nothing but means they have been dehumanized, it turned into nothing but tools to be utilized to get what you want in any way possible simply because you want that result. Ultimately, despite the immorality of the behavior, you will do whatever it is that you must get the result you wish to only because it will get you what you want, and that is all you care about at the end of the day.

These people should never be trusted—they always have an ulterior motive, no matter how truthful they may seem in the moment. There is always something motivating them to behave in specific ways; whether it is innocent or not is up for debate. You are better off avoiding and not trusting this person whenever possible.

Narcissism

The other one is the narcissist—those with narcissism have a narcissistic personality disorder. It is characterized when an individual present with a grandiose sense of self, meaning he is quite egotistical and believes that he is far superior to a pervasive lack of empathy and an excessive need for admiration and attention. The narcissist thrives off of getting his or her sense of self-justified through actions such as praise or admiration—they only see themselves as worthwhile if others around see them as worthwhile first. They want to be recognized as worthy and will do whatever it takes to get that.

It means that narcissists are often willing to lie about who they are or what they like. They have no true sense of self beyond someone that desperately seeks the approval and admiration of others, no matter what the cost, and is willing to do whatever it takes to get it, even if that means lying about who they are.

The narcissist typically creates an alter ego of sorts, a persona that he presents to the world that is everything he wishes he was—charismatic, powerful, influential, and well-liked. He then utilizes several dark psychology manipulation techniques to keep people under the spell he seeks to create. He creates a sense of self and then always plays mind games and manipulates those around him. Only those who get close to the narcissist to be trapped in his web of lies beyond hope of getting out ever see his true self. The malicious individual lies beneath the persona, lurking for the first possible chance to lash out at those around him.

After snaring a victim within his trap, he will systematically manipulate the other person, conditioning them into doing whatever the narcissist desires. Over time, he can mold his victim into the perfect source of constant admiration, something referred to as his narcissistic supply. He will then always utilize manipulation and mind control techniques to keep his new toy under his thumb for as long as possible, attempting to break down his victim by any means necessary systematically.

Psychopathy

Psychopaths suffer from their personality disorders, in which they are often characterized through a series of persistent antisocial actions. They almost always lack any real sense of empathy—the innate human ability to connect emotionally with others at any meaningful level. This lack of empathy makes them incredibly dangerous. Without empathy, which is a built-in red flag system that lets us understand when something is wrong with those around us, particularly in regards to our behaviors to others, the psychopath has no real fail-safe to his or her behaviors—he will continue to push and push, even with the most aggressive behaviors, simply because he does not feel any need to stop. For those who do feel empathy, the pain they, themselves, feel as they harm someone else is usually enough to make them stop. The pain and guilt become overwhelming, and they stop before making it worse. The psychopath, however, does not feel that.

Beyond the lack of empathy and, therefore, remorse, psychopaths typically exhibit disinhibited behaviors—in simpler words, they are impulsive. A thought will pop into their mind with some random impulse, such as stealing a purse from someone or deciding to hurt another person, and they are far more likely to act upon it simply because they like to act upon their impulses.

Psychopaths are frequently also bold—they do not fear anything they are approached with. Consequences are not intimidating. People are not intimidating. Even dying or being harmed is not intimidating to the psychopath. The psychopath is incredibly tolerant of danger and is frequently noticed to have high confidence and assertiveness. Even though he is not likely to want to do anything meaningful with that confidence—he sees no point in engaging in social conventions.

The Dark Triad

With those three personality types now described in an easy-to-understand manner, you may now be wondering what happens when the three are combined. The results are an aggressive, toxic individual who does not care to act in a normal manner. They are fantastic at exploitation, lacking the empathy necessary to impede such negative, harmful behavior, and having the right amount of lack of impulse control to encourage it. They manipulate, they hurt, they steal, and they lie. They are callous, meaning they do not care about others' feelings and revel in seeing people hurt, angry, or sad. Research has shown that people with the dark triad personality type all enjoyed seeing people with negative expressions on their faces.

Ultimately, those possessing the dark triad are not forces to be reckoned with—they will do anything that will hurt you if you wrong them, and they do not care enough about social conventions to be held back from seriously harming you.

Chapter 2. How To Analyze People

It is the knowledge of the character by the features of the face and hand. It is about moving from an empirical art to an observation science. The character is not independent of the physical constitution. The state of our body conditions it. On the other hand, the body is influenced by the emotions of the soul.

Life is due to a double movement: a dilation movement and a conservation movement, which analyzes any human being's personality.

The Dilation-Expansion

Its adaptability characterizes it to the environment, an externalization of intuitive and affective tendencies, sociability, cheerful humor, need to be in groups, intelligence adapted to the useful and directed to practical realizations.

The Conservation-Seclusion

Oppositely manifests itself, with an elective adaptation to a privileged environment. Since withdrawal is a defense process, it acts only in a medium that does not suit you.

While the expansive individual is a friend of the whole world, disperses his activity in all directions, reacts impulsively, is determined, and has a sensory intelligence of immediate contact, the withdrawn has only friends of choice. If he does not have them, he prefers loneliness, concentrates, and is only active in some directions. It is not resolved unless he has reflected, does not trust his sensory impressions, and is more idealistic, replacing reality with abstractions, distrusting his senses, and reason.

The Expansive Individual

It is characterized by having a thick structure, colored and warm skin, wide round face, largemouth, snub nose, large eyes, and a smiling expression, with ease and abundance of exchanges.

The Retracted Individual

It is thin in nature, short limbs, dry and cold skin, and pale dye. The face is elongated, narrow, and bony. It is economical, selective in the exchanges, smallmouth, narrow and bony nose, sunken eyes, hermetic face, and little communicative.

The Expansive-Retracted

It is an intermediate of the recent two; the face is rectangular, large eyes slightly sunken. It opens or closes, depending on the situation.

Physiological Tricks to Analyzing People

In valuing people we have just met, we are often victims of our psychological mechanisms. It can lead to misunderstandings and preconceptions that eventually affect our ability to socialize. The best way to counteract these mistakes is to know how to identify them, so here are the common mistakes we make when valuing others.

Confuse Personality and Situations

When we observe someone's specific behavior, we immediately think that they act according to their personality. Instead, when we think about our behavior, we usually value it based on the situation in which we find ourselves.

For example, we know that we are distant when we are worried about something. However, if a person you just met acts in this way, you may directly assume that he is a jerk. To avoid falling into this trap, we should always consider the so-called situational conditions when valuing other people.

Confirmation Bias

Once we have a specific idea about someone, we usually see everything they do through the filter of these preconceptions. For example, if you consider a co-worker to be selfish, you look at the behaviors that confirm it, but not those who deny it.

Although our first impressions are usually quite reliable, they are not infallible, so it is essential to consider our judgments as we continue to relate to that person. The best way to prevent confirmation bias is to seek evidence that challenges your initial assumptions actively. Psychology calls this process "positive DE confirmation of expectations."

The Wavy Effect

The wavy effect is a cognitive bias whereby we make a generalization wrong from a person's single characteristic. The variable that most causes this effect is physical attractiveness; that is, we tend to value those who seem attractive to us more positively. Similarly, we also tend to value better those who resemble us.

An effective way to understand how it works is to identify when it occurs in critical situations. For example, when you hire someone for a job or when you are in a situation that involves many new people. If we pay attention, we will see that, in both cases, we tend to gravitate towards those people with whom we share certain features, whether physical or cultural background.

Let Us Influence the Past

A bad experience with a postal officer can lead us to assess all civil servants negatively. In the same way, knowing a person who reminds us of someone from our past can influence our judgment about that new person. For example, if the most undesirable person in your class at the school was named Alberto, you will have more difficulty positively assessing a person with that name.

One way to avoid this negative influence is to pay attention to our reactions' proportionality and identify when we approach a situation with a negative or defensive attitude.

The Supposed Similarity Bias

Usually, we tend to assume that others think like us and have our same preferences. But obviously, this is a mistake. If you want to skip this type of cognitive prejudice is to create a habit of warning people about diversity in people's preferences and expectations. That is, allow people to let you know that their comfort zone is different from yours.

Secrets of How to Analyze a Person

You surely wanted to be able to read the minds of other people more than once. With the aid of their formed instincts, some are spared, but if you are not so wise, you have only one way out: learn to decode the body's language.

It's no longer a secret that we get 55% of the information with the aid of non-verbal communication. Face expressions, emotions, and actions of the body will strip anyone's disguise and reveal their true thoughts and feelings.

Closing Your Eyes

If a person closes his eyes, talking to you, you must know that he is trying to hide or protect himself from the outside world. That doesn't mean I'm scared of you. Alternatively, the other way around, He wants to take you out of his dream area. You may already have bored it. Open and bam your head! You're done.

Protecting the Mouth by Hand

It's a vivid example from childhood that we all come. Remember, when you didn't want to say anything, you covered your mouth with the palm of your hand. It's the same person. Many fingertips, fist, or palm allow us to express the words. Sometimes with a feigned cough, we mask it.

Biting the Rim of Your Glasses

Does your buddy intentionally bite his glasses rings? Try to encourage and support him. He must surely be concerned about something, and he wants to feel safe at his subconscious level, as in childhood with the mother's breast. By the way, the same applies to a pencil, pad, finger, cigarette, or even chewing gum in hand.

Stroking the Chin

The person is trying to decide this way. Your attention can be focused downwards, sideways, to the left, or any other side at the same time. He doesn't know what he sees at that exact moment because he's immersed in his feelings.

Crossed Arms

One of the most repeated movements. It is not shocking that many people feel very comfortable with this posture, as this gesture helps separate themselves from others. When we're not happy with something, we use it several times. The crossed arms are a clear sign of your interlocutor's negative attitude.

Self-Exposure

This posture is more accessible, right? When a woman wants to like a friend, by revealing her best sides, she starts to reveal herself. She straightens and bends her thighs to show her breasts. The folded arms below are a clear signal of the interlocutor's attention.

Leaning Forward

Normally, he leans forward when a person feels concerned for their interlocutor and needs to contact him or her. The feet that remain in the same place at the same time, but the body moves unconsciously.

Leaning Back

If the individual leans against his seat's back, he clarifies that the conversation is boring. In your interlocutor's company, you can feel uncomfortable.

Handshake "Glove"

It indicates you can trust him if your interlocutor embraces you with both paws.

Squeeze with Palm Up

The palm-up displays sensitivity, protecting the interlocutor's face, but only if achieved at once. If the hands were already holding for a particular moment, and then somebody placed the hand palm up, it may signify a desire to show who is in charge.

Squeeze with a Touch

The person can touch the forearm, elbow, or back of the person he greets with a single hand. This personal space invasion shows the need for contact. And the smaller the body becomes, the more important it is.

Straightening the Bond

It depends on the situation here. If it's a man who does it in a woman's presence, he may very much like it. But this gesture can also mean the person is not feeling comfortable. You may have been lying or just wanting to leave.

Collecting Non-Existent Hair

The gesture of repression is thus called. We use it most of the time to express their overt dissatisfaction. We don't express their opinion freely, in other words, but we certainly disagree with what's going on around them.

Feet on the Table

This expression can mean many things: bad manners, arrogance, the desire to show off as a great boss, or health concern. Nonetheless, psychologists tend to believe that it would be safer to use it at home or in your relatives' company, even if you are very confident in this role.

Riding the Chair

A chair is not a saddle, and the back is not a shield, although it seems to be in some respects. It was also designed for other uses. This way of sitting around is troubling so many people, so we feel a lot of hostility from the "hung" individual at the intuitive level. Powerful men usually use this position.

Eye Contact

The eyes are the soul's mirror as well as a natural interactive device. There we can read all the interlocutor's feelings and emotions. Lovers look at each other's heads, expecting unintentionally to see how they get larger. And this shows a lot as, relative to their normal state, the pupils will increase in size up to four times. By the way, if the person gets mad, their eyes become like accounts because of the pupils' full reduction.

Chapter 3. Speed Reading to Understand People

If you are ready to read other people, then this is the guide for you. Ultimately, being able to read other people is highly essential. If you want to understand what is going on in someone else's mind, you need to tell what is going on with their bodies first. The truth is, people are quite easy to learn to read if you know what you are doing. All you have to do is make sure that you are looking at specific clusters.

Ultimately, we all communicate with people in different ways. We have both verbal and non-verbal signals that we give off at all times. However, the bulk of our communication is non-verbal. We have plenty of body language that we use in different ways to understand what is going on with other people. We look at proximity to each other and general demeanor to figure out what is going on inside one person's mind to get more information from them. When you do this, you learn to recognize how you can interpret what they are about to do, if they are going to do anything at all.

Within this guide, we will take a look at what it will take for you to begin understanding other people at a glance. You will learn how to understand the basic expressions, attraction, closed behavior, assertiveness, and dominance. All of these are important in their ways, serving essential roles that you can utilize. All you have to do is make sure that you know what to look for!

Reading Expressions

Ultimately, we have seven primary expressions—these are known as our universal expressions because you can spot them pretty much in any culture. Every one of us knows what a smile is, and you can recognize it immediately. That is because a smile is an expression that is considered universal. Let's look at the six universal emotions now so that you can better see what to expect with them.

Happiness

Happiness is easy to understand. When you see someone that's happy, you can recognize it by the smile primarily. However, the most obvious sign of happiness is the crinkle in the eyes—this is how you know that the smile and happiness are legitimate.

Sadness

When it comes to sadness, you can identify it by the fact that the entire face melts. You can see that the eyebrows go down. The corners of the mouth do as well, and the inner corners of the brows go up. There may or may not be crying involved as well.

Anger

Anger is defined by three primary characteristics, aside from the demeanor that goes with it. Usually, someone who is angry will have their brows lowered while pressing their lips together firmly. Alternatively, the mouth may be open, bearing teeth and squared.

Fear

Fear is usually shown as brows up high on the face, but still flat, with the eyes widened. The mouth usually opens widely as well.

Surprise

The surprise is similar to fear in people, but the marked difference is that the jaw lowers alongside the mouth's opening, and the eyes are usually opened wider, showing whites on both sides. The brows are also arched instead of just raised.

Disgust

Disgust is noticed primarily by taking a look at how the face comes together. The upper lip goes up, rising slightly. The nose bridge usually wrinkles as well, and the cheeks pinch in and up to try to protect the eyes.

Reading Attraction

When a person is attracted to someone else, they show undeniable body language as well. In particular, you can expect to see all sorts of specific actions. The body does not usually lie, and because of that, you can look directly at the behaviors that someone is doing to figure out if they are attracted to you or not. In particular, you want to look for the following behaviors:

Sustained Eye Contact

You will see that the other person will maintain eye contact more when attracted to you. Additionally, they will usually look away and then glance right back to see if you're still watching them.

Smiling

There is a reason we assume smiling is flirting—it happens often. The flirty, attracted smile usually lasts longer and includes flirty eye contact, and fleeting, but regular.

Self-grooming

Men and women both do this—they brush their hair with their hands, adjust their clothes, and otherwise tamper with their appearance when they are flirting or talking to someone they find attractive. If they do this regularly, they may be attracted to you.

Looking Nervous

Being nervous is a very normal thing when attracted to someone else, and this usually shows itself through fiddling with something repeatedly.

Leaning in

Typically, people will lean toward things that they are attracted to, and people are no exception to that rule. You will also notice that the feet will point at the person that the individual is attracted to.

Licking the lips

This is a common one, but it is subtle and easy to miss. However, you can notice it if you pay close attention. Usually, it is noticeable by a quick part of the lips and a small suck or lick.

Reading Assertiveness

Assertiveness is calm, confident, and in control. Effectively, if someone is assertive, they behave as if they are in control—they take charge, are comfortable with themselves, and won't go out of their way to overstep on other people. They sit back and allow things to play out without letting anyone else dominate them. The most common signs of assertiveness include:

Smooth Body Movements

When you are assertive over something, you don't have jerky movements. They are smooth and in control without much of a problem, even when energized or emotional. The voice sounds smooth as well, and they slowly and steadily look about.

Balanced

The assertive individual is usually upright, relaxed, but also well balanced and comfortable.

Open Body Language

Usually, these people will show that they are open to engagement without threatening or provocative. They do not block off their bodies at all and show open hands as well.

Eye Contact Regularly

Eye contact is usually steady and maintained comfortably without much of a problem.

Smiling

There are plenty of polite smiles and listening well with this body language as well. Usually, you can expect the other person to be quite comfortable, and they will smile efficiently and appropriately.

Firm

While they are firm, they usually have a solid stance without much of a problem. They are not confrontational and typically show that they are willing to listen, but they are also firm. They do not escalate anything and tend to avoid aggression in any form.

Reading Domination

Domination is a little more than assertiveness. Usually, with assertiveness, you see someone that is showing that they are confident without being threatening. However, with dominance, you can expect to see a much more threatening demeanor. A dominating body is going to show signs such as:

Facial Aggressiveness

You will be able to see the aggression in the face—usually in the form of frowning and sneering or even snarling.

Starring

The aggressive individual will usually stare at someone they don't like or may also squint or attempt to avoid looking at someone entirely.

Widebody Stance

They will usually stand out with their shoulders widened and may even hold their arms wide open as well. They may also stand with their hands placed firmly on their hips in a crotch display.

You may notice sudden movements that the aggressor is very rough with his movements, moving about suddenly and even erratically sometimes. It is a good sign that they are not in a perfect spot and may do something else aggressive.

Large Gestures

You may notice that as the individual moves, he will signal with aggressive, almost too big or wide movements that get close to you without ever getting close enough to touch you.

Reading Closed Behavior

Finally, let's go over closed behavior before we continue. Closed behavior shows that the individual is not interested in engaging with the other party at all. When you see closed behavior, you know that the individual will not want to engage with you; you will see that they want to be left alone. You can expect to see symptoms or signs of this sort of behavior, such as:

Crossed Arms

This is perhaps the most telltale sign. When someone feels closed off, they will almost always cross their arms and keep their hands near their bodies. When they speak during this time, they will keep a monotone voice. Think as your sign that you create a barrier between yourself and the other party with your arms. You want to be alone, so you close yourself off entirely.

Crossed Legs

You can also cross off legs as well—when you do this, you see that the knees are across from each other when sitting down, or they can cross the ankles as well. It creates an even more closed off image that shows that you are defensive and unwilling to listen or change your viewpoint on something.

Looking Away

It is also prevalent to see that the closed-off person wants nothing to do with those around them. They don't want to look at the person that is engaging with them.

Leaning Away

You may also see that the closed-off person wants nothing to do with getting close to the individual engaging with them either.

Instead, they will pull away and lean back, trying to put as much distance between them as possible.

Feet Turned Away

Look to the feet when you want to know how engaged someone else is. If you see that the other person is standing away, feet pointing away from you, they are closed off and don't want to engage in the conversation at all.

Chapter 4. Advanced Tips and Tricks to Control People

So you're playing the seduction game and leading someone to get intimidated by you? Again, manipulation is a powerful weapon in your arsenal that can be used negatively or positively to achieve your objectives with the person, even though it may have largely negative connotations. There are plenty of psychological tricks that can be used to get close to a person or lead them to be intimate with you.

Exercise due caution and diligence when it comes to using these techniques because your dignity and reputation are at stake here. Playing with other people's emotions always to have your way will make you come across as distrustful, deceptive, and selfish.

Flattery

Flattery is a brilliant way to break the ice with someone you've just met or lead someone you know for ages to do what you want. Ensure that you disguise flattery (however fake it is) in the garb of genuine and specific compliments.

For example, instead of telling someone how lovely they look in a particular piece of clothing, say something like, "I love how the color of your eyes is beautifully complemented by what you are wearing." It sounds more genuine and invariably draws the person to you.

There is a secret strategy when it comes to resorting to flattery. Identify an area where the person is slightly insecure and needs reassurance. Use specific compliments related to that area to win over the person. For instance, if someone has issues related to speaking confidently in public, tell them that they have a wonderful voice texture or always use the right words while talking. It directly squashes their concerns and insecurities and makes them feel nice about an area they aren't too sure about.

Make Them Indebted to You

It is another slightly insidious strategy that can be used to seduce a person or get them to do what you want. It is a universal strategy that is effective across cultures, classes, and genders. You make the subject feel indebted to you by doing them a series of favors. In their mind, they become obliged to you even though they didn't ask for it.

You create a misbalanced equation where you are the giver, and they are the receiver. To make the equation more balanced, they know they have to pay you back in some form. Take advantage of this titled balance and get them to do what you want by straightforwardly asking them when the time comes. There are high chances the person has already mentally conditioned himself or herself to pay you back. Evil as it sounds, the tactic is used by several people who will fund others' lifestyles to make them feel indebted to the manipulator. The subtext is, "I own you because I pay for everything you use." It may start with small things that the subject voluntarily opts for, which then becomes impossible to get out of.

Use Shame or Guilt

There's no denying that the manipulation seduction game can get sneaky and complicated with blurred right and wrong lines. However, the manipulator widely uses another technique to charm people into going out or sleeping with them. It comprises inducing feelings of guilt or shame on the subject.

If the manipulator's requests are continuously turned down, he or she will make the subject feel guilty or shameful about refusing them. For example, "You know how lonely I am, living all alone away from my family. I've had a very rough and lonely childhood where no one ever loved or cared for me. You are also adding to my feelings of being lonely and uncared for with your cold and disinterested attitude. I know the world is against me, and no one wants me."

Manipulators know how to induce feelings of guilt by pushing the right emotional buttons. You will make more sweeping statements (no one loves me, the world is against me, or I've had a rough childhood) rather than state-specific instances. Manipulators cleverly study what makes the other person feel guilty and target those areas to get what they want.

Another disturbing yet highly successful seduction manipulation technique is to make the other person feel shameful about their past actions repeatedly. Though it may help you get what you want in the short run, it will certainly not set the basis for a healthy, rewarding, and meaningful relationship in the future.

Steer the Conversation

Seducers who've mastered the art of manipulation will almost always hold the remote control of a conversation to lead their subject into doing what they want. For example, if you want to sweet talk with a date, spouse, crush, or friend who is nagging you about something, you steer the course of the conversation by changing the topic to a more favorable one.

"Hey, I just saw a gorgeous blue, low-cut outfit that would look flattering on you at Mary Ann's boutique the other day" or "I saw the most jaw-droppingly beautiful house at Lakeview Lane on my way to work the other day, what do you think about living there together?" It takes the conversation from a rather unpleasant tone into a more welcoming and inviting tone that sets the pace for wooing someone or triggering feelings of intimacy in them.

False Logic

Teens and adolescents mostly use this one, but there's no denying that plenty of adults resort to it too. The logical fallacy or false logic creation technique comprises creating a seemingly false argument and making it sound that it is indeed true. When you tell someone that if a particular thing is true, they will not do something that you deem undesirable.

For example, "if you love me, you will get married to me immediately" or "if you trust me, you won't hesitate to go to bed with me" You are challenging them to prove their feelings and emotions by getting them to do what you want them to.

Make it Appear Normal

So what you as a manipulator are doing here is making the subject feel like what you've asked for or what you want them to do is normal. To do this, you stealthily use numbers, statistics, and research findings for your advantage. You make someone feel like they think differently, while what you are asking for is normal. This way, they are led into believing that something is wrong with their thinking.

For example, "statistics reveal that 75% of people end up sleeping with each other right after the first date." You establish that it's a norm and that most people would do it, and they are crazy or abnormal if they think otherwise.

Silent Treatment

Seduction experts using manipulation know how to use the silent treatment all too well. It works like magic when you're getting someone to obey your wishes. When you remain silent, it impacts the other person by making them feel like they have done something wrong or hurtful.

They become even more eager to make up for it when they realize that you are hurt, angry, or upset with their actions.

The Mirror Effect

As someone who uses the mirror effect manipulation technique for seducing the subject, you attempt to establish a level of trust and emotional comfort by convincing the other person that you are exactly like them. The manipulator pretends to have the same background, values, interests, personality traits as the subject. You may also share fake stories, secrets, or confessions to build a sense of trust, familiarity, and emotional proximity with the other person. You let them know what they want to hear emotionally, and they return the favor with what you do to them, often sexual.

It is the basis of most seduction-manipulation techniques. Manipulate someone's emotions to lead them to think and feel in a particular way, and then get them to bed with you.

Create a Compelling Want

Seduction is all about creating a compelling desire and then presenting yourself as the source for fulfilling it. It is pretty much what every advertiser, salesperson, and internet marketer use.

They create a specific thing in their prospective clients' lives and then present their products or services as the only solution.

Build a strong need for what you have to offer. Make them feel like they need you to fulfill their physical and emotional objectives. Do not be afraid to show them how you can help them or what you can offer them. Strut your strengths and tease until they are convinced that you've got what they need!

Maintain a little distance from the subject to show them what they desire is slightly out of their reach. They will be yearning for you more when they realize that you have everything they want and are yet out of their reach. It makes them strive for your attention even harder!

Chapter 5. The Most Powerful Mind-Power Tool

Humans spend countless hours seeking new ways to work just about anything. Through endless hours of research, they pour over books and journals looking for the message that will tell them the secret to harnessing mind power. Many never realize that the most powerful mind power tool is already on board and just aching to be used. It is the human brain, the mind itself.

Every time a person practices a new habit or thinks a new thought, they make a new pathway in the brain. Every time the habit is used, or the idea is thought, the nerve pathway becomes even stronger. The human brain is wired at birth to be an efficient machine, and it is ready, from birth, to make an ever-increasing amount of nerve pathways and strengthen the pathways used the most.

Sometimes thoughts and habits need to be changed for the improvement of the person. When people decide that they would like to change their lives, there will be a period of adjustment. It is true whether the change is mental, emotional, or physical. During this period of adjustment, there will be some level of discomfort. When a habit or a thought is already formed, it has made its path in the brain. When a stimulus is seen or heard, the message travels along the preset nerve pathway to the brain's spot that controls that thought or habit. To change a thought or a habit, the nerve path must be changed. Until the nerve path is changed, the old nerve path will remain in the brain. The brain's discomfort is trying to access the old pathway, and the new pathway simultaneously automatically. It is painful for the brain to do.

It is easy to become frustrated when the brain goes back to its old thought and habit patterns. Never fall into the habit of placing blame on a lack of willpower. Willpower has nothing to do with it. It is a challenging thing to override preset pathways in the brain. The brain is a very powerful tool. When will power fail, and mistakes happen, always remember to use kindness and compassion to deal with the failure? The brain is very efficient at doing what it does. The only way to change the brain's pathways is to keep working on new pathways that will eventually obliterate the old, undesirable ones.

The brain needs a clear understanding that changes are about to occur, and new pathways are about to be laid down. Remind the brain that new habits and new thoughts will be replacing the old ones. Blaming failure on a lack of willpower is a self-defeating statement. The process of making new nerve paths in the brain takes hard work and time. It will help to keep reminding oneself of the impending change. By doing this over and over, it makes the process no longer about possible character flaws. The focus is now put on the habit of thought that is being built.

Is it possible to build new nerve pathways in the brain? Yes, it is possible, and it can be done. If more proof is needed, compare the adult brain to the baby's brain. Every current habit and thought a person has the direct result of practicing them repeatedly until they created a brain pathway. New pathways can be created. The baby's brain has no idea of anything. It has no thoughts or habits. Every nerve path currently in the brain was practiced until it became a part of the brain. Think of the baby. The baby lies around day after day and does baby things. Then one day, the baby notices the shiny rattle that mommy is waving in front of its little face. The baby wants the rattle. As the baby is waving its tiny arms around, the mommy puts the rattle close enough so the baby can touch it with its wavering hand. After a few of these sessions, the baby gets the idea that it can touch the rattle if the arm is in the air. A nerve pathway is beginning to grow. So the baby decides to lift its arm to reach for the rattle actively. The baby will be unsuccessful because the arms will wave wildly and will not connect with the rattle. One day, the baby will grab the rattle, and the nerve pathway is then complete.

While this may seem like a straightforward example, it is precisely how nerve pathways are created in the brain. Every action, thought, or habit has its nerve pathway. All pathways must be created. No one was born knowing to sit in front of the television and mindlessly eat dip with chips. No one was born lamenting the excess pounds they carry in strange places. No one was born hating their body; all behaviors are learned, good and bad. And the bad ones can be replaced with good ones.

So if the ability to program negative thoughts into the brain exists, then the ability to disrupt those negative thoughts with positive thoughts also exists. The brain can be reprogrammed. It is a powerful tool, and its main function is to turn thoughts into reality. The brain is always working, so why not use the brain's power to benefit rather than harm? Just because a particular habit or thought has been around forever, it does not mean it needs to stay. Use the brain's power to choose new habits and thoughts to focus on and replace the brain's old, negative thought pathways.

The new thought needs to be believable; the new habit needs to be doable. It does not look really good to try to stick to a habit that is impossible to accomplish or to try to believe an unbelievable thought. After years of seeing an obese body's reality, it would be nearly impossible to suddenly believe that the mirror image is that of a skinny person. But the brain will likely accept something that mentions learning to take care of the body or learning to accept the body to correct its flaws. The brain will turn a belief into reality. Believing a positive thought will lead to a different result than the ending where only negative thoughts are present.

Be prepared to repeat and repeat some more. The primary key to being able to make a new habit stay is repeating it constantly. The more a new, desirable habit is practiced, the more the brain begins to accept it. The nerve path becomes stronger every day. With constant practice, this new nerve path will become the path the brain will prefer to use, and the old one will cease to exist.

In any case, be sure to allow enough time to create a change effectively. Accept the starting point and continuously visualize the ending point. Accept that the path to the goal of a new habit or thought will not be easy or perfect. The path will rarely travel in a straight line. Sometimes people fall entirely off the path, and that is okay too. Do not get sidetracked by the idea that this journey will be comfortable and carefree because it will not be. Just keep thinking of the new nerve pathway created by the new thought or habit, and it will eventually become a reality.

Most of the pathways in the brain are stored in the subconscious mind. It is the part of the mind that is always working without always being thought of. Think of learned skills like tying shoes, zipping a coat, and pouring milk into a glass. These were all learned behavior whose nerve pathways are firmly set in the subconscious part of the mind. This part of the brain is the bank of data for all life functions.

The communication between the conscious mind and the unconscious mind works in both directions. Whenever a person has a memory, and emotion, or an idea, it is rooted in the subconscious mind and translated to the conscious mind through mind power. The subconscious has the power to control just about anything a human regularly does.

For example, during meditation, steady, deep breathing is usually practiced. The control of the breath is brought from the subconscious mind and given to the conscious mind to control the breathing. Once a pattern of deep, steady breathing is begun by the conscious mind, the subconscious mind takes over and keeps the set rhythm going until it is told to stop. It is done by a conscious end to deep breathing. The subconscious mind also processes the great wealth of information received daily and only passes along to the conscious mind those necessary for the brain to remember.

When sending thoughts from the conscious mind to the subconscious mind, the brain will only send those thoughts attached to great emotion. The only thoughts that remain in the subconscious are those that are kept there with strong emotions. Unfortunately, the brain does not know the difference between positive emotions and negative emotions. Any strong emotion will work. Both negative emotions and positive emotions can be quite strong. Also, unfortunately, negative emotions tend to be stronger than positive emotions.

Step one in learning to use the subconscious part of the mind's power will be to eliminate any thoughts that come with negative emotions. Also, negative mental comments will need to cease. Fears will usually come true, precisely because they are drowning in negative emotion. Negative ideas need to be eliminated because they can be very harmful roadblocks on the road to harnessing brainpower.

One best practice to use to get rid of negative thoughts is to counter them with positive thoughts. It will take time and practice, but it is a very powerful and useful technique. Whenever a negative thought pops in the conscious mind, immediately counter it with a positive thought dripping with strong emotion. The actual truth will come out somewhere in between the two thoughts.

Another way to counter negative emotions is to delete them, just like using a remote control. When a negative thought comes into the conscious mind, imagine destroying it. Imagine writing that thought on paper and burning it. Imagine pointing a remote control at the thought and pressing a huge delete button. Whatever form used to imagine deleting the thought, the important thing is to get rid of it before taking hold in the subconscious mind.

Find something energizing and use it to reach a goal. Those things that are found to be energizing bring boundless energy to positive thoughts. It is often necessary to invent motivation to learn to create new habits and thoughts, at least in the beginning. But with a bit of practice and a lot of positive thought, new positive habits will soon be burned into the subconscious mind, and the old negative thoughts and habits will fade away.

Chapter 6. NLP

You learned all about NLP, persuasion, and other subjects connected to these two. Remember all of the body languages you were taught—out of everything, that maybe one of the best skills to foster and develop. You learned of several different ways people can control, influence, and persuade other people to do what they want or need. You learned all about how people prefer to interact with others and genuinely and naturally develop the persuasion and influence that so many people desire. You were also taught how to develop several social skills that are of the utmost importance if you wish to be successful.

Ultimately, the information should guide your behaviors. Let this allow you to go through your life, be informed, and aware of how your behaviors influence others. Focus on those around you with their body language and see how easily your behaviors can sway them. Learn from negotiation skills to ensure that you can get what you want while still giving back to others. Remember how to keep your interactions with those around you ethical, even if you understand how to take over and manipulate them into obedience to do whatever it is you are seeking.

Neuro-linguistic Programming practitioners and trainers have put forward exemplary approaches and techniques to persuade, which can be used in various environments. Studies state that these techniques develop personal performances and help the individual maintain good intrapersonal and interpersonal relationships.

To persuade someone entails a process of altering and rebuilding their opinions, beliefs, values, and behaviors towards an outcome. Humans are programmed to find it extremely difficult to move out of their comfort zone, no matter their comfort zone. For some individuals, even if their comfort is unhealthy, they wouldn't mind staying in it because, well, it's comfortable.

Persuasion is just not about forcing an individual to behave how we want them to behave; it is about allowing them to come out of their comfort zone to achieve a higher comfort zone after the discomfort of the change subsides. Simply put, an individual who regularly smokes will keep smoking because it is his comfort zone. To persuade or convince him will be a pretty challenging task because quitting is uncomfortable for the person. During the non-smoking period, this person might go through considerable discomfort. Still, afterward, he will experience a higher comfort zone due to the absence of his unhealthy behavior.

For persuasion to be successful, the person tries to persuade the individual to figure out what is essential to the individual. The persuader should identify factors that can eventually give the individual a higher level of comfort. For a person who finds staying at home and shunning social life comforting, the persuader should discover a factor that can allow them to move outside the box. By helping them realize that although going out can be, they will have a higher sense of comfort once they achieve their goals. This process needs a skilled persuader to assure the client that the behavior change will make them feel more comfortable.

Advantages of NLP

These NLP techniques can increase the level of influence that you exert on others. Companies that engage in marketing and sales depend entirely on persuading their clients or clients to buy their products; the strategies presented in NLP guide these sellers and dealers to increase the chance of influencing their clients in making decisions. NLP also increases the person's performance; NLP helps you modify and replace your negative behaviors with more positive ones. These strategies also help you to improve your leadership style. Being humble and non-judgmental allows you to have a better communication style, even outside the persuasion process.

Essentials for Persuasion

Empathy

This is an essential quality that a persuader requires. You should not only be thinking about yourself, but you also should try to put yourself in the other person's shoes and think about how they might be feeling. Empathy also helps deter you from being judgmental.

Listening Skills

Only a good listener will persuade another person; a person who is always ready for an argument will never be a good listener. If you want to be a good and positive persuader, you need to listen to what the other individual says and pay attention to their body language.

Indirect and Clever Commands

People tend to be more responsive to suggestions than questions. For example, instead of using the words "Would you like to go to the concert?" You can say "Come, let's go to the concert"; this motivates a more positive response from the individual.

Restrict the Choices That You Provide

Try not to allow the individual to say "No." Taking the same example, instead of asking, "Will you be able to stay long at the concert?" ask them, "Would you like to stay here for three hours or four?" The latter question makes it hard for the individual to say a "No."

Allow the Person to Visualize

Successful persuaders always help the client, or the individual visualize to convince them. An example would be, "this concert will make us scream the lyrics of our favorite songs."

Always Make It Simple as Possible

Trying to convince the other person by bragging will only be a failure; keep it as simple as possible and remember you should never put their views down.

You can use the information you were provided for good. You can use it to better your relationships, your career, and your social life. If you understand how people interact with others, you can ensure that you are interacting positively. You can make every interaction with other people positive and fulfilling for everyone involved. Above all, you can naturally develop the skills you need to create and earn your leadership skills. People will naturally seek to follow you if you build your NLP and persuasion techniques. People will listen to you better if you have advanced social skills. You can use it to your advantage to ensure that you and those around you are happy with life. Use your enlightenment and knowledge for good, and go out there, armed with the knowledge you need to persuade others, both for your benefit and theirs.

So, what are you still waiting for? It is time to embrace this guide so that you'll allow the light inside you to radiate without fear of hurting others of being all that you are meant to be. This guide will help you overcome manipulation so that you can shine brighter!

Chapter 7. Covert Manipulation

Numerous people in the world do not realize that mind control has become a dangerous aspect used by different people to control others and resources. Mind control is used in different aspects of life, and the list below might surprise you by the extent to which it has expanded in modern-day life. When we think of mind control, some of us assume that it is a direct way of getting into the brain and influencing the very mechanism in which we think. However, mind control is much greater than that, and its effects are putting control of the world in a few elite hands.

It is necessary to consider how agencies, companies, and even individuals practice mind control, as it is an important aspect of NLP manipulation. Mind control is basic to begin with, but it can also be complex in practice because different people use different aspects of technology to control those around them. The following list is but a taste of the different approaches to mind control in the world.

Mind Control with NLP for Love and Relationships

We will learn what truly good and fulfilling relationships are based on and built upon. We will explore techniques that can strengthen relationships and those that can help us establish healthy relationships. Many factors play a role in good relationships. We will discuss the importance of our mental health and readiness before entering into any partnership or relationship, and possible outcomes associated with having and not having these factors.

We all want and need certain things. There are basic needs for all of us, and one of the most crucial ways we can have our basic emotional needs met is with healthy relationships. We all want to be loved, desired and needed. We all long for compassion and understanding. All of these can be acquired in good and healthy partnerships. Likewise, a bad relationship can be devastating. Most of us carry around baggage, such as negative emotions, fear, and anxiety from previous unhealthy relationships. This can place barriers between us and others when we find ourselves in new relationships. True fulfillment usually can only be found in the emotional qualities of our relationships.

Every good relationship begins with a clear and comfortable frame and state of mind. The maturity of both parties is a factor, as well as timing. Your goals and wants need to be compatible with the person you want as a partner. Your values and beliefs need to match. These ideas and characteristics are tangible and very important in the overall health of any relationship. If you find yourself in a great relationship, the benefits are numerous. You will gain confidence and a feeling of self-worth that can't be matched. Just as important, you must also remember to transmit this to your partner. You should always treat your partner exactly the way you want to be treated. In doing this, and having this knowledge, you can know what it is that your partner wants. You just need to see what it is that your partner is doing and take it from there.

Before we can be the kind of partner we should, we must first be good within ourselves. If you enter into a relationship, while you have self-doubt or internal difficulties, you are entering a partnership that is doomed from the start. A perfect couple consists of two people who can function well as individuals but function as a partner just as well, if not better. This is the first step in entering any relationship. You must be good with yourself. This is a must and shouldn't ever be compromised. The second important point that needs to be addressed is establishing what, or who, it is that you desire. This is your personal decision based on your personality, desires, ideologies, and belief system. It does not matter what others believe you need or what you think you should have. What matters is what you want.

The next part of entering into a good relationship is timing. This isn't just important to you, but it's also important with your partner. Are you looking for "Mr. Right" or "Mr. Right Now?" Are there things going on currently in your life that may prohibit your success in the relationship? Are these things not only able to hinder you, but are they able to hinder your partner as well? Timing is important and crucial to the longevity of the relationship. If you are a point in your life where other priorities take precedence with you, you should wait until those priorities shift. You can become capable of making your partner the priority that he or she deserves.

Once you have decided what you want, have concluded that now is the time for you to enter into a relationship, and have covered all of your predetermining factors. Now you can begin to open up to the possibilities of finding the right person. Here is when rapport becomes important. What is rapport? It's your similarities and likeness with someone with whom you are interested in entering a relationship. It's also the establishment of trust with that person. With rapport, many individual factors can be used for determining compatibility. Some of these are personality types, values, beliefs, culture, political ideologies, interests, religious beliefs, etc. Of course, physical characteristics, such as gender and body types, need to be considered. However, some characteristics can't be over accentuated because it will mimic the other and cause a loss of rapport.

The rapport established in the beginning, the reasons for your attraction to your partner, and his or her attraction to you must be kept at the forefront of each partner's mind throughout the relationship. It all too common for people to enter into relationships with guns blazing, meaning being the perfect partner, only to begin to relax and change once the relationship has been established. One partner, or both, will use all available techniques to get the other to enter into a relationship. Once they are in that relationship, the other partner believes they can initially tone down what they were doing. This is one of the most common reasons for relationships ending. Keep in mind; the reasons for someone falling for you are the same reasons that will make them want to stay with you. If you remove the reasons for their attraction, they have no reasons to stay with you. Often, we see children born of relationships used as new reasons, but this does not work. This leads the partnership to morph into what can be seen as a business relationship. There will be no real emotional connection in the relationship and, even though that couple may remain together, they will lack the comforts and fulfillment of needs they desire.

Now you have identified what you want, making sure the timing is right, and have met that special someone. Now, what do you do? You need to make sure that your partner feels the same about you. There are several ways in which a person can see that they are loved by the other. These ways should be identified at the relationships beginning. A few methods are by what the other person buys and place him, or she takes you. There are also things such as how they touch you, the looks they give, or what they say. Identification of these is important as they can gauge the continuance of love throughout the relationship.

The best way to determine how you can best assure your partner that you love him or her is by doing what they tend to do for you. For instance, most likely, if your partner puts her arm around you at times to assure you of her love and affection, you can bet that if you do the same, she will believe that you do love and appreciate her. We don't tend to do things to or for others, especially those whom we care about the most, that we wouldn't want to be done to us. Although this is commons sense, it's also a great method to gauge or determine how your significant other feels about you. As the relationship progresses, this will come naturally and will take much less conscious effort. Just be sure not to allow these things to stop because the relationship is no longer new.

NLP has devised a few strategies to determine areas in relationships. Areas such as attraction, love, and desire are all strategized with NLP techniques. First, you must know your partner. This means that you should know what those subtle gestures and tones of voice your partner will display depending on how they feel. Know what your partner fears and what he or she wants. You will pick up ideas as to how to carry these things out simply by learning your partner. Be sure never to use this knowledge for manipulation. There isn't a positive outcome in relationships where manipulation takes place.

One technique you can use to ensure that your partner is in love with you and wants you is to remove yourself from his or her presence temporarily. This does not mean that you can tell your wife that you are going to the store for a lottery ticket to not return for a week. However, in short time frames, absence can signal want or lack thereof. Just like the cliché, absence makes the heart grow fonder; this is built on the same premise. When using these kinds of tactics, please never overuse them. Here is some advice. If you are an insecure person needing constant approval and reassurance that you are loved, you should take care of that issue before entering into a serious relationship.

If not, you are not going to be a good partner. If your shortcoming does not end the relationship, it could lead it to become a codependent partnership or, at the very least, a very unhealthy relationship. Again, you must first make sure that you are a good candidate for entering into a relationship before taking that other step.

With relationships, you are not simply selling yourself to another, and then the job is over. It's a continuing process forever. Never relax and believe that you have your partner, and he or she isn't going anywhere, no matter what you may or may not do.

Many divorcees have made this mistake countless times. You should always be selling yourself, your worth, compassion, and desire for your partner.

Chapter 8. What is Manipulation?

When coming from a psychological point of reference, manipulation is mostly about perception. How we perceive things or actions determines our laws, social formalities, and even our lives.

The manipulator changes these norms with tactics. The determination of the positive or negative connotation of these actions remains subjective. Psychological manipulation is often considered devious. With the subject of dark psychology, we can take into account that the manipulation practiced is often exploitative at the expense of others.

So, what is the manipulation of the dark?

Sources tell us that it is concealment—hiding in the shadows knowing when to strike. It is also a false front, hiding true intentions. When we are talking about this level of deception, we are talking about hiding aggression. When we take, there is a certain level of aggressive behavior that happens. A small part of manipulation is hiding that aggressive behavior so that the victim sees only good nature.

This is accomplished in various ways and means, one being knowledge. When we allow another to know us, we display vulnerability along with strengths. The knowledge of these personality traits can give the manipulator the ability to maneuver around without any alarms going off.

The effectiveness of manipulating those strengths and vulnerabilities arrives when the dark practitioner knows what is vulnerable and what inspires pride.

A reoccurring ideology that drives us to war takes into consideration that war is more negative than positive. We want to avoid it. The manipulation process sees pride in all of us and plays to that pride. It is our strength. However, when used to drive an army to slaughter others, the intention of our pride has been manipulated to enforce the agendas of others.

There is ruthlessness when we talk about psychological manipulation. When dealing with someone other than the pure psychopath who feels little to nothing, ruthlessness can be measured. Often soft ruthless behavior can sneak up on its prey and snag it before it knows what is happening. This harm of the prey becomes less than even a momentary qualm in the mind of the manipulator.

Often the practitioners of dark psychology use aggression and fear to drive us. The less dark side still falls into the category of knowing what weakness is, and that weakness leaves the individual open to control.

How the manipulator uses that control determines the severity of manipulation. There are positive versions of manipulating others, such as convincing someone that they are not doing well and need help. However, we are looking at the darker side of this. The manipulator uses their control skills to get what they want—and the cost does not apply.

There are many ways to move another into a place of being controlled. From the positive to the negative, psychological manipulators utilize all tactics.

When positive reinforcement is used, the charm is displayed. A forced smile or laughter can trigger laughter in all of us. As when we were infants, we copy what we see. When we see tears, we want them to stop. When we see a smile, we find ourselves smiling as well.

Using positive reinforcement, the manipulator can shower money, charm, and gifts to get us to feel something. The usage of these things allows control of us on an instinctual level. We follow those who tell us what we want to hear.

Psychological manipulation can also implement negative reinforcement. This is a form of deflection—a substitution of one thing for another.

Often, we have things we need or have to do, and we do not really want to do them. The psychological manipulation of negative reinforcement uses that power of negativity to lure the subject from their original need, pushing them toward something they want to be done instead. The long game, a slow play of putting tasks into another's life and then controlling those tasks, so that the manipulator can get what they want, is an extremely effective and subdued tactic.

Sometimes only partial reinforcement is required to gain control. We are talking about elevating the fear or doubt regarding the tasks needed to be done. The partial is the long play. It knows that in the end, the victim will lose. It knows that by planting small seeds now, victory will eventually happen. It knows that we all have our weaknesses and that by planting even a small seed, we can take someone to that weakness. An individual trying to work toward something they already were shaky on or had doubts about, will listen to the lie and flow with that idea, and use it to their own destruction.

The partial manipulator only needs to put the thought in mind, knowing the weakness is already there and utilizing it will take their prey to a destructive end.

Psychological manipulators flat, outright punish. From an actual physical lashing to the victim's passive-aggressive playing, punishment is very effective when one wants to control another.

We skulk, cry, yell, nag, and go completely silent. This is the blackmail of the manipulator. It inspires guilt in us. That "wanting to be the better person" rises to the front, and we do what the manipulator wants.

When the manipulator sets free the crocodile tears, we have no idea if they are real or not. The degree of crying is not up to us to determine. Only the manipulator knows if the tears are legitimate or not.

In this case, the trap is often sprung from the victim's side. They walk up to the hurt individual to help, only to find that the manipulator is just lying in wait to strike.

One extreme version of manipulation is violence.

Violence triggers something inside us. We often do anything to avoid it. The manipulator knows that violence strategically applied can make us go into a state of avoidance. There incites the control. Physical violence can have mental scarring. The manipulator causes the scarring. It places violence in tactical places to get the result they want.

Some would say this is the darkest of the dark.

Taken to the individual, this can mentally damage them for a long period of time, if not permanently. Placed on a world stage, it can lead all the way up to the physical conflict of genocide.

The manipulation process in dark psychology is normally not a single move. It is a complex series of moves, often with the outcome only known by the manipulator. The motivations of manipulators are as convoluted as human nature.

Mostly it is about gain. Manipulators of the dark want to gain something. When we speak about gain, we are talking about power and influence, control and manipulation over others. The trophy is up to the individual. This can be everything as to gaining affections, to money, and even to life itself.

It is about gaining for their own personal reasons and gratifications. The taking of others and making the power and control their own. Selfishness to the extreme. The mind of the dark practitioner sees the ultimate win as gain over others.

They have power. Superiority is the power over another, and taking of someone else's power makes them feel superior. This is a huge driving force behind the manipulator. Often, in the case of immature individuals driving manipulations toward superiority, any is pushed aside for just the feeling of being superior.

In relationships, it is about control. The manipulation of power can put one in control. Although we have looked at the role of the vampire and power, and we know who really has control.

This feeling of control can be overwhelming to the mental state of the dark. Almost drug-like, it is a feeling of emotion that is most logical. Control is one of the easiest manipulation tactics to achieve with only logic to guide. It drives not only the victim but the manipulator as well.

Psychological manipulation can also be about self-esteem. The self of the manipulator is always in question. This is one of the reasons they manipulate, to define themselves. How easily they are able to manipulate another can tell the dark that they are better than others. That weakness and strength can be measured in the tactical playing field of the hustle.

This defines who they are. Can they manipulate? Yes? They are stronger. No? They are weaker. It is a measuring device for self-esteem.

However, we are not saying it is the only device for measurement. Self-esteem can be measured by far less damaging means.

The mind gets bored, and what do we do when we get bored? We seek entertainment. How do we achieve entertainment? We manipulate.

We all do it.

Let us assume we are bored, and we want to remove or alleviate that boredom with something else. Do we just sit back and wait for something new to happen?

No. We actively search for something to replace boredom. Manipulation can take place on many different levels, as well as the severity of which they are applied, from picking up a crayon and coloring to taking a mental absence to massacre everyone around you.

The dark psychological manipulator is bored most of the time more than most. The psychological manipulator will often use manipulation to determine their own validity of feelings and emotions.

What this boils down to is that manipulation applied in relations with others helps the manipulator to regulate reactions to validate or not validate their own emotions. The manipulator measures the self and their self-esteem by how others handle their personal self-questioning.

This happens when the practitioner does not have a grasp on what emotions are. They look at their own emotions as invalid and manipulate the situation in such a way as to validate them.

We are stuck with ourselves, and we cannot get away. Psychological manipulators validate or invalidate themselves by the tactical controlling of others. It is an interesting way of viewing life, although there is one form of manipulation that we all idolize—the con. One common form of manipulation is convincing of another to make their money yours.

This is a hidden agenda of the criminal. This form of mental manipulation preys mostly on the elderly and the rich. However, we all can fall to this form of manipulation. What we choose to spend on and what we do not is our response to a form of psychological manipulation.

Something happens when the buck is passed over. We go from manipulation into action. Something drives us. It is within us, and it is outside forces that drive. What causes this drive and the drive itself is called persuasion.

Chapter 9. Examples of Manipulation?

It is worth noting that manipulative people don't always come out of nowhere. Often we find individuals with this behavior in the workplace, at school, and in the family. The characteristics presented above are shaped according to the mode of friendliness. Here's how to deal with manipulative people in these environments:

At Work

In a professional environment, the manipulator is the employee always ready to help, but remember, it's compulsive help. He stays at the heels of colleagues, reinforcing how much he loves helping colleagues who have difficulties in their tasks. The manipulator on the desktop can stay up and even take a break in the office, all for the "pleasure of helping others." The targets of "goodwill" are charmed with such dedication.

The manipulator is seen as the company's legal person, employee, and fellow stick to for all work. However, this establishes a relationship of dependence. Whoever is the target of "goodwill" is being placed on the web. The one who receives the "help" loses his autonomy since he cannot act without asking for the manipulator's opinion. Consequently, he loses confidence and does everything not to lose this "friendship." When the victim begins to perceive himself as such and tries to escape, the manipulator reverses the roles and convinces his prey that he is bad. The prey, in turn, accepts such a condition and follows the will of his tormentor.

How to Get Rid of the Manipulator at Work?

Be firm and kindly dispense unsolicited favors. When the manipulator takes the day off to flatter you, return the compliments, but make it clear that you are just doing your duty, and anyone else would do the same. The manipulator will be amazed at your steadiness.

In School

At school, the manipulator is the perfect colleague. The manipulator targets unpopular students who are constantly ridiculed.

The manipulator praises the high notes. You are sure that the "new friend" is the best student. When his grades are low, he places the teacher's blame because the teacher certainly did it to harm him. He does not hesitate to defend injustice. There is no bad time that prevents you from helping with the activities, and the manipulator makes a point of doing the work with you. The target of such unknowing friendship reveals what time he leaves home, what time it takes to drive there, reveals possible enmities with other students, tells of his fears and anguish. The manipulator reveals nothing about his life.

When the victim realizes that something is strange and tries to disengage, the manipulator feels extremely offended. He places the "friend" as an unjust person, unable to recognize true friendship. The manipulator depreciates the "friend," listing his defects, and claims that he will return to being a solitary person and be ridiculed if the friendship ends. The prey, who already had low self-esteem, is even more vulnerable. Thus, the victim believes the manipulator, apologizes, and no longer measures their efforts to do all the manipulator's will, so afraid of losing the "friendship."

How to Get Rid of the Manipulator in School?

If you feel that you are being cheated again, move away slowly. Speak only as necessary and ask other people's opinions on how to deal with the situation.

In the Family

In the family, the manipulator sticks close to that shy relative and is considered good by everyone. It may be that cousin who always compliments, even when the victim has done something that isn't so great. The manipulator justifies his "object of affection" blockades and believes that his target is wrong. He insists on telling us how much he loves us and is happy to be with such special people.

The manipulator is always ready to go to the mall, help with school activities, go to the doctor's office, and do some repairs. However, when the target begins to be bothered by the excessive clinginess and flattery, the manipulator turns the tables and lowers his victim. The manipulator underscores his lack of social skills and how he is seen as lonely, poor, and a failure unable to have friends. The sentences that the victim says will continue to be seen as unimportant. The already emotionally unstable target agrees with everything, apologizes, and resumes "friendship," doing everything according to his tormentor's will, afraid of not being able to count on such a valuable person.

How to Get Rid of the Manipulator in the Family?

Family ties make things harder, but we must put an end to this vicious circle. Ask the opinion of people outside the family spectrum. Even if it is not possible to cut the manipulator out of the conversation, talk only when necessary.

Differences Between Male and Female Manipulators

The behavior between men and women is different in several respects. On the question of manipulation, there are also singularities.

Men

Male manipulators have the following characteristics:

- Shy: the manipulator observes the behavior of everyone around him. He transmits fragility and submission to convince himself that he is a needy person.

- Handsome: manipulators are always friendly, extroverted, and know how to live life. They show extremely worried and attentive with their "friends," but they make a point of showing who is in charge. The victims do not feel the courage to disagree with such a nice man, but when he goes to a boring event, he does not bother to disguise his boredom.

- Altruist: he gives many gifts, does numerous favors, always intending to receive something in return. When it is not "reattributed," it gives people a sense of guilt.

- Seductive: vain and attractive. He looks into others' eyes, asks embarrassing questions, and loves to make a mystery of himself.

- Worship: has excessive admiration for diplomas, pompous professional curricula, and social projection. He subtly shows contempt for those who do not have the same knowledge. He loves to embarrass people, monopolizes conversations, and gets annoyed when someone interrupts his speech.

Women

Manipulative women behave in the following ways:

- In front of everyone, they are true porcelain dolls. However, when the target moves away, she's stupid with people. When the victim returns, she will be candid with him/her.

- Use beauty as a weapon to get what she wants. It seems absurd to someone not to praise it.

- She uses a sensual tone of voice and promises a thousand wonders to those who satisfy her requests; she wants the target to guess her wishes and surprise her with trips, restaurants, and luxury gifts. She becomes angry if her requests are not answered.

- Her emotions can be radical. When you are right, she wants to prove that it's better that you are wrong. When she is wrong, she does not admit it and insists until someone believes in her.

- They cry too much. If the victim wants to go out with other people, she cries because she was "betrayed." If she is asked how the car got scratched, she cries because she was accused of being a bad driver. She is "fragile" to the point of not carrying a suitcase or not being able to open the car door.

Manipulative people enter our lives because they see that we are going through a moment of vulnerability. We feed these people by providing intimate information. However, if we allow them to enter our lives, it is up to us to remove them from the scene. The task is difficult, but these tips can be useful:

Do not feel guilty for not satisfying the wishes of the manipulator. Often they are irrational and seem like things a child who wants attention at any cost may request. Ask probing questions; question what will change if you attend to the manipulator's wishes. Ask yourself how your feelings were before and how they are now. Learn not to speak to those who do not do you good; this means you must avoid saying yes to the manipulator.

If none of this works out, move away. If it is not possible to physically get the person out of your life, move away emotionally, and speak only about the basics. Remember that manipulative people are "toxic people," non-evolved beings who want to suck energy and steal others' autonomy. No one deserves to live in the shadow of others. No one deserves to live, having to consult someone at every step. Emotional independence is the key to a happy existence.

Conclusion

What is Deception?

How can deception be defined? Deception, alongside subterfuge, mystification, feign, deceit, and beguilement, is an art employed by an agent to spread beliefs in the subject, which are untrue, or truths coated with lies. Deception involves numerous things, for example, dissimulation, sleight of mind, suppression, cover-up, propaganda, etc. The agents win the subjects' favor; they trust him and are unsuspecting of his propensity to be dubious. He can control the subject's mind having won their confidence and trust. The subjects have no doubts about the agent's words. The subjects trust the agent completely and possibly plan their affairs based on the agent's statements.

The deception practiced by the agent can have serious consequential effects if discovered by the subjects. How? The subjects will not be disposed to hearing his words; neither will they accept them anymore; no wonder the agent must be skilled at the deception technique. He must create an escape route to cover up if things boomerang and still retain the trust his subjects have in him.

Deception breaks the laws that govern relationships, and it has been known to affect negatively the hopes that come with relationships. Deception does occur now and then, resulting in feelings of doubt and disloyalty among the two people in the relationship. Nearly everyone desires to have an honest discussion with their partner. However, if they find out that their partner has been dishonest, they, in turn, need to find out how to make use of confusion and distraction to get the reliable and honest information that they require. On the other hand, the trust would be lost in the relationship, making it hard to restore the relationship to its former glory.

The individual on the receiving end of both dishonesty and betrayal would always wonder about the things their partner was telling them, thinking about whether the story was true or false. As a result of this new doubt, most relationships will be brought to an end once the agent realizes their partner's dishonesty.

Types of Deception

Deception is a type of communication-based on omissions and falsehood to convince the world's subject that best fits the agent. There is a need for communication to occur. There will likewise be various kinds of deception. As per the Interpersonal Deception Theory, there are five different sorts of deception. A few of these have been revealed in other types of mind control, showing some similarities.

The five major types of deception include:

1. Lies: this occurs when the agent manufactures information or provides information that is not similar to the truth. They will give this information to the unsuspecting individual as the truth, and the individual will then see this lie to be fact indeed. However, this can be unsafe as the person being given this false information would have no idea about the falsehood. Most likely, if the subject understood that they were being given information that was not true, they would not be on talking terms with the agent, and no deception would have occurred.

2. Equivocations: this is the point at which the agent will make statements that are differing, unclear, or not direct, such that the subject becomes confused and does not understand what is going on. Also, it can help the agent to preserve their reputation, saving face if the subject returns to blame them for the falsehood.

3. Concealments: it is the most frequently used form of deception. It refers to when the agent leaves out information related to or critical to the situation on purpose or displays any such behavior that would cover up information important to the subject for that exact situation. The agent won't have lied straightforwardly to the subject. However, they will ensure that the vital information required never gets to the subject.

4. Exaggeration: occurs when the agent emphasizes too much on a fact or stretch the truth just a little to twist the story to suit them. Although the agent may not directly be lying to the subject, they will manipulate the situation such that it appears as though it is a bigger deal than it is, or they may twist the truth to make the subject do whatever they need them to do.

5. Understatements: this is the inverse of the exaggeration tool in the sense that the agent will present part of the fact as less important, telling the subject that an event is less of a deal, than it is when it really could be what decides whether the subject gets the opportunity to graduate or gets a huge promotion. As such, the agent will return to the subject, saying they had no idea how huge a deal their omission was. They get to keep their reputation, leaving the subject to look petty if they protest.

The above are only some of the forms of deception that there are. The agent of deception will use any means available to reach their final goal, the same as what happens in other types of mind control. However, these methods mentioned are not limiting, as the agent would use any means to get to their goal.

The agent of deception (who will be good at what he does) can be dangerous since the subject will not know the truth or lie.

Reasons for Deception

It has been confirmed by researchers that there are three major reasons for deceptions found in intimate relationships. These motives focused on the partner, on self-image, and focused on a relationship.

In the case of the partner-focused motives, the agent will use deception to keep their partner from harm. They could also use falsehood to save their partner's relationship with an outsider, thereby protecting the subject from worry or keeping the subject's confidence intact. This reason for the deception is often seen to be of benefit to the relationship and socially respectful.

In comparison with some of the other reasons for deception, this one is not as bad. If the agent finds out something terrible that the subject's closest friend said about them, the agent might remain quiet about it. Although this is a type of deception, it not only saves the subject's friendship but also keeps the subject from feeling terrible for themselves. This is the type of deception that is often found in most relationships and also, if found out, might not cause a lot of damage. To protect their partner, a larger percentage of couples would use this form of deception to protect their partner.

The self-focused motive for deception is not thought to be as noble as the partner-focused motive for deception, and as such, is not as acceptable as the other methods. Rather than stressing over the subject and how they are doing, the agent is going to simply consider how they are doing and about their very own self-image. Here, the agent uses deception to protect the agent from criticism, shame, or anger. Using this form of deception in a relationship is typically seen as a serious issue and offense than in partner-focused deception. This is because the agent chooses to act in a self-centered manner instead of protecting their relationship or partner.

Lastly, in the relationship-focused motive of deception, the agent uses deception to prevent any harm coming to the relationship, basically staying away from deception, relational disturbance, and quarrel. This type of deception will either help or harm the relationship, depending on the circumstances. This form of deception could be harmful because it makes things rather complex. For instance, if you do not reveal just how you feel about dinner to prevent a quarrel, this might just help the relationship. If you keep to yourself that you took part in an extra-marital relationship, the situation is only going to become more complex.

No matter the motive of deception in the relationship, deception is not advised. The agent is holding back details that may be vital to the subject; when the subject discovers it, distrust in the agent will set in, and they are left to ponder what other details the agent is keeping from them. However, the subject would not be too worried about the reason behind the deception. They will simply be vexed that they have not been told some things, causing a split in the relationship. Usually, it is best to stick with truthfulness in the relationship and not encircle yourself with individuals who don't put deception into practice in your social circle.

Detecting Deception

An individual interested in preventing deception from avoiding the mind games that come with it should learn how to detect deception when it occurs. It is not usually easy to know when deception is going on, as there are no pointers to rely on, except the agent makes a mistake and either tells an obvious lie or says something that the subject knows to be false. While it might be difficult for the agent to mislead the subject for a long time, it will usually happen regularly between individuals who know one another.

Deception can place a heavyweight on the agent's cognitive thinking because they will need to find a way to remember all their conversations with the subject on the situation. Hence, the story stays believable and dependable. Any mistake will bring the subject to the realization they are being deceived. The stress involved in keeping the story believable is much, and as such, the agent is very much likely to spill out details that will give the subject a clue that they are being deceived either through nonverbal or verbal signs.

Researchers believe that detecting deception is a process that is cognitive, fluid, and complicated and will regularly differ based on the message that is being passed across. As indicated by the Interpersonal Deception Theory, deception is an iterative and dynamic process of influence between the agent, who attempts to manipulate the information and how they need it with the goal that it varies from the truth, and the subject, who will at that point try to know if the message is true or false. The agent's activities will be concerning the actions that the subject makes after they get the information. Through this trade, the agent will uncover the nonverbal and verbal information that will signal the subject into the deceit. Eventually, the subject might have the capacity to tell that the agent has been lying to them.